Take Me To Your Liter
Science and Math Jokes

Take Me To Your Liter
Science and Math Jokes

Compiled by Charles Keller
Illustrated by Gregory Filling

A TRUMPET CLUB SPECIAL EDITION

ISBN 0-590-23000-X

Text copyright © 1991 by Charles Keller.
Illustrations copyright © 1991 by Gregory Filling.
All rights reserved. Published by Scholastic Inc., 555 Broadway, New York, NY 10012, by arrangement with Pippin Press.
TRUMPET and the TRUMPET logo are registered trademarks of Scholastic Inc.

12 11 10 9 8 7 6 5 4 3 2 1   7 8 9/9 0 1 2/0

Printed in the U.S.A.

For Nicole and Leigh

What do Martians who use the metric system say?
"Take me to your liter."

What do you call a math teacher with his head in the clouds?
Pi in the sky.

What did one raindrop say to the other?
"Two's company and three's a cloud."

Why was 6 afraid of 7?
Because 7 ate 9.

Use the word "geometry" in a sentence.
When the little acorn grew up it said, "Gee-I'm-a-tree."

I've discovered a liquid that can melt anything.
That's great.
The only problem is I can't find anything to put it in.

What does a hungry math teacher like to eat?
A square meal.

Your telescope magnifies only three times.
Oh, no! I've already used it twice.

What's the difference between maximum and minimum?
When Maxi won't talk, that's maximum; when Mini won't talk, that's minimum.

Do you like my new plant?
What kind is it?
It belongs to the rose family.
I thought you said it was yours.

What did Benjamin Franklin say when he discovered electricity?
Nothing. He was too shocked.

What is the best way to pass a geometry test?
Know all the angles.

Who invented fractions?
King Henry the Eighth.

Why did the man go to the reptile house on opening day?
He wanted to get a snake preview.

What did the limestone say to the geologist?
"Don't take me for granite."

What did you write your science report on?
A piece of paper.

What grows larger the more you take away from it?
A hole.

If April showers bring May flowers, what do May flowers bring?
June bugs.

To succeed in math you must have self-confidence. You must avoid phrases like "I can't." Do you think you can do that?
I can't see why not.

Newton was a famous scientist. He founded Newton's law.
Boy, that's some coincidence!

What is one-half of one-tenth?
I don't know, but it can't be much.

Dad, where is the Big Dipper?
Ask your mother. She puts everything away.

What's raised in Brazil during the rainy season?
Umbrellas.

If you had ten dollars and gave away one quarter, another quarter and then another quarter, what would you have left?
Ten dollars minus three quarters.

What sign were you born under?
Maternity ward.

Science homework is for the birds.
Yes, but if you don't do it you're a dead duck.

What is a polygon?
A lost parrot.

How does a child ghost count?
One, boo, three.

Mom, what would you do if I got a 100 on my math test?
I'd probably faint.
That's what I thought. So I settled for a 75.

If it takes five men fifteen hours to build a brick wall, how long would it take ten men to do it?
Why should they build it at all? The five men just did it!

Why is your January math grade so low?
Things are always marked down after Christmas.

There are three people under one umbrella and none of them get wet. How come?
It isn't raining.

What does a good-looking triangle have?
Acute angle.

Is it true that the law of gravity keeps us from falling off the earth?
Yes.
What did we do before the law was passed?

What did one math book say to the other?
"Don't bother me. I have my own problems."

What's the fastest thing in the world?
A shadow. Nobody's ever caught one.

Why is the ocean salty?
Because fish don't like pepper.

Do you know what an echo is?
Can you repeat the question?

What flowers are the laziest?
The ones in bed.

Let me hear you count.
1,2,3,4,5,6,7,8,9,10, Jack, Queen, King.

You copied Mike's math test, didn't you?
Yes, but how did you know?
Because on one question Mike wrote, "I don't know," and you wrote, "Me, neither."

If you had $5 and you asked your mother for $5, how much would you have?
I'd have $5.
You don't know your math.
You don't know my mother.

What kind of skates does a calculator wear?
Figure skates.

How many paws does a lion have?
One pa and one ma.

Did you see the plant in the math teacher's room?
No, what about it?
It's growing square roots.

Billy, what do we call the last teeth we get?
False teeth.

How are you doing in your math course?
I'm working really hard to get ahead.
That's good. You could certainly use one.

What did Mrs. Edison say to Thomas?
I don't know, what?
Tom, I don't care what you invented. I can't sleep with that light on.

What colors would you paint the sun and the wind?
The sun rose and the wind blue.

I saw something last night I couldn't get over.
What was it?
The moon.

What can you tell me about nitrates?
They're cheaper than day rates.

Can you tell me something about seventeenth-century chemists?
Yes, they're all dead.

What is a bacteria?
The rear entrance to a cafeteria.

What did the Little Dipper say to the Big Dipper?
"I want to be a big star when I grow up."

What is measured by the yard but worn by the feet?
A carpet.

Why does the ocean roar?
You would too if you had lobsters in your bed.

What's the longest piece of furniture?
The multiplication table.

Who adds, subtracts, multiplies and bumps into light bulbs?
A mothematician.

How are the rain and the snow similar?
Rain comes in sheets and snow in blankets.

Why do soccer players get good grades in math?
Because they know how to use their heads.

What is the best way to make a fire with two sticks?
Make sure one of them is a match.

What did one geologist say to the other?
"Are you going to the rock festival?"

What's the difference between the land and the ocean?
The land is dirty, but the ocean is tide-y.

Do you believe you can move objects with your mind?
Sure. All I have to do is think about catching the school bus and it pulls away.

When do mathematicians die?
When their number is up.

If you tear a piece of paper into four pieces, what do you get?
Quarters.
Right, and if you tear a piece of paper into eight pieces?
Eighths.
And into a million pieces?
Confetti.

Did you know that every time someone breathes, someone dies?
Have they tried mouthwash?

I spent eight hours over my math book last night.
You did? How come?
It fell under my bed.

When does a math teacher wear dark glasses?
When she has bright pupils.

I don't think I deserve a zero on my math paper.
I don't either, but it's the lowest mark I have.

If you have twelve oranges and give away three, how many would you have?
I don't know. In my school we do arithmetic with apples.

What is a net profit?
What a fisherman earns.

What did one decimal say to the other?
"Did you get the point?"

Dad, could you help me find the least common denominator in this problem?
Don't tell me they haven't found it yet. They were looking for it when I was a boy.

If you had ten potatoes and had to divide them among five people, how would you do it?
I'd mash them.

What is the chemical name for water?
H-I-J-K-L-M-N-O.
Who told you that?
You did. You said it was H to O.

Why are numbers one to twelve good detectives?
Because they are always on the watch.

Why do lions eat raw meat?
Because they aren't good cooks.

Add up the following: one ton of sawdust, four loose screws and twenty nuts and bolts. Got all of that in your head?

Yes.

I thought so.

Look at the great books I have on plants.

Where did you get them?

At a branch library.

Why isn't your nose 12 inches long?
Because then it would be a foot.

Teacher, would you punish me for something I didn't do?
No, why?
I didn't do my math homework.

How many feet are in a yard?
That depends on how big the yard is.

Is it true that lightning never strikes twice in the same place?
Yes, after it strikes once, the place isn't there anymore.

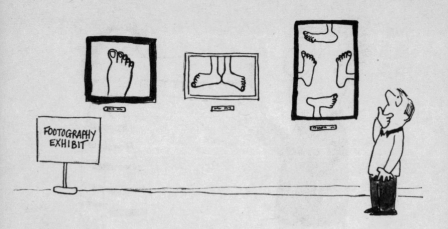

What do you call a picture of a foot?
A footograph.

Did you hear about the angry inchworm?
No.
He had to convert to the metric system.

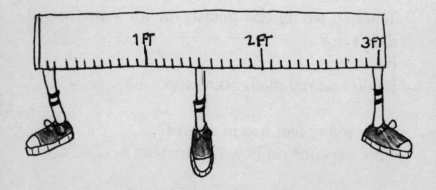

What has a foot at each end and a foot in the middle?
A yardstick.

My teacher said we would have a test today, rain or shine.
Then why are you so happy?
Because it's snowing.

If you have your tonsils removed it's called a tonsillectomy.
Okay.
And if your appendix is removed it's called an appendectomy.
Okay.
And if you have a growth removed from the top of your head, what is it called?
A haircut.

What would you have if you had 37 apples, 8 pears and 46 bananas?
A fruit stand.

How many sides does a box have?
Two—the inside and the outside.

What did the calculator say to the cashier?
"You can count on me."

What do you call a list of hurricane names?
A gust list.

Do you know that eagles have such keen eyesight that they can read a newspaper from a mile away?
Wow! I didn't even know they could read.

What runs and runs but never gets anywhere?
A clock.

Our math teacher talks to herself.
So does ours, but she thinks we're listening.

We have the Stone Age and the Iron Age.
Name another.
The saus-age.

What is a hydroplane?
When you order a hydro without lettuce or tomato.

Some plants have animal names like dogwood and cattail. Can you give me another example?
Sure—collie-flower.

If you put your hand into one pocket and found seventy-five cents and then put your hand into your other pocket and found twenty-five cents, what would you have?
Somebody else's pants on.

Did you know that it takes three sheep to make one sweater.
No. I didn't know they could knit.

Did you know they laughed when Edison invented the steamboat?
Fulton invented the steamboat.
No wonder they laughed.

Your science homework looks like your mother's handwriting.
I used her pen.

Mom, would you do my arithmetic for me?
No, it wouldn't be right.
Couldn't you try anyway?

What number has its own day?
Two's day.

Why does lightning strike people?
Because it doesn't know how to conduct itself.

Name a flower you can't pick.
The Mayflower.

Can owls see better at night?
Yes, but they have trouble holding the flashlight.

If you laid a mile of pennies in a straight line what would they add up to?
A sore back.

Why are the sunrise and the sunset so dangerous?
Because they are the times when day breaks and night falls.

Do you think paper can be used effectively to keep people warm?
I sure do. My last report card kept my family boiling for a week.

When the rain falls, when does it go back up again?
In dew time.

If I took three apples from a basket that contained twenty apples, what would you have?
If you took three apples, I'd have three apples.

I just invented a metric cookie.
Great.
I'm going to call it the "gram cracker."

What is at the end of the rainbow?
The letter "W."

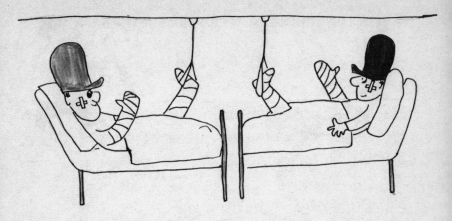

Two trains are at the opposite ends of a railroad track 100 miles long. One engineer is traveling at 50 miles an hour and the other is traveling at 40 miles an hour. Where will they meet?
In a hospital.

Who helped invent the telephone and had a cookie name after him?
Alexander Graham Cookie.

Why did the brilliant scientist disconnect his doorbell?
To win the No-Bel Prize.

What musician is most likely to get struck by lightning?
The conductor.

If you faint, what number will revive you?
They'll have to bring you 2.

What is 5 plus 5?
10.
And what's 5Q plus 5Q?
10Q.
You're welcome.

If you add 362, 47 and 184, subtract 29 and then divide by 7, what would you get?
The wrong answer.

What's the difference between electricity and lightning?
You don't have to pay for lightning.

You should get good marks in geometry.
Why?
You're a square and you talk in circles.